365 DAY
BRIGHTENERS

For

Women

By

Women

365 DAY BRIGHTENERS

FOR Women
BY Women

GARBORG'S
because every day is a gift

*O*nly a night from old to new,
Only a sleep from night to morn.
The new is but the old come true,
Each sunrise sees a new year born.

HELEN HUNT JACKSON,
1830-1855, American writer

He put a new song in my mouth,
A hymn of praise to our God.
Many will see and fear
And put their trust in the Lord.

PSALM 40:3 NIV

*J*ANUARY 1

JANUARY 2

How much of our lives are...well... so daily. How often our hours are filled with the mundane, seemingly unimportant things that have to be done, whether at home or work. These very "daily" tasks could become a celebration of praise. "It is through consecration," someone has said, "that drudgery is made divine."

GIGI GRAHAM TCHIVIDJIAN, 1945- ,
American writer, speaker, d. Billy Graham

A joyful heart is like a sunshine
of God's love, the hope of eternal
happiness, a burning flame of God....
And if we pray, we will become
that sunshine of God's love—
in our own home, the place where
we live, and in the world at large.

MOTHER TERESA OF CALCUTTA,
1910-1997, Roman Catholic nun, Nobel Peace Prize winner

*J*ANUARY 3

JANUARY 4

*N*one of us knows what the
next change is going to be,
what unexpected opportunity
is just around the corner, waiting
to change all the tenor of our lives.

KATHLEEN NORRIS,
1947- , American writer

I avoid looking forward
or backward, and try to
keep looking upward.

CHARLOTTE BRONTË,
1816-1855, British writer

If I rise on the wings of the dawn,
if I settle on the far side of the sea,
even there your hand will guide me,
your right hand will hold me fast.

PSALM 139:9-10 NIV

*J*ANUARY 5

JANUARY 6

*G*od bless you and utterly satisfy
your heart...with Himself.

AMY CARMICHAEL,
1867-1951, Irish missionary to India, poet

I know that God is faithful. I know
that He answers prayers, many times
in ways I may not understand.

SHEILA WALSH,
Contemporary, American singer, speaker

JANUARY 7

JANUARY 8

I do not ask for any crown
But that which all may win;
Nor try to conquer any world
Except the one within.

LOUISA MAY ALCOTT,
1832-1888, American writer

*A*ll my life through, the new sights
of nature made me rejoice like a child.

MARIE CURIE,
1867-1934, Polish-born French physicist

*J*ANUARY 9

JANUARY 10

Live your life while you have it.
Life is a splendid gift—
there is nothing small about it.

FLORENCE NIGHTINGALE,
1820-1910, British nurse, hospital reformer

*Give away your life; you'll find life given back,
but not merely given back—given back with
bonus and blessing. Giving, not getting, is the
way. Generosity begets generosity.*

LUKE 6:38 THE MESSAGE

*F*ace your deficiencies and acknowledge them; but do not let them master you. Let them teach you patience, sweetness, insight. When we do the best we can, we never know what miracle is wrought in our life, or in the life of another.

HELEN KELLER,
1919-1985, American writer, crusader for the handicapped

*J*ANUARY 11

JANUARY 12

*E*verything which relates to God is infinite. We must therefore, while we keep our hearts humble, keep our aims high. Our highest services are indeed but finite, imperfect. But as God is unlimited in goodness, He should have our unlimited love.

HANNAH MORE,
1745-1833, British writer, social reformer

*L*ook at a day when you are
supremely satisfied at the end....
It's when you've had everything
to do and you've done it.

MARGARET THATCHER,
1925- , former Prime Minister of Great Britain

*J*ANUARY 13

JANUARY 14

There is nothing I would
not do for those who are really
my friends. I have no notion
of loving people by halves.

JANE AUSTEN,
1775-1817, British writer

I am not afraid...
I was born to do this.

JOAN OF ARC,
1412-1431, French patriot and martyr

*No test or temptation that comes your way
is beyond the course of what others have
had to face. All you need to remember is
that God will never let you down; he'll never
let you be pushed past your limit; he'll always
be there to help you come through it.*

1 CORINTHIANS 10:13 THE MESSAGE

*J*ANUARY 15

JANUARY 16

Courage is the price that life exacts for granting peace. The soul that knows it not, knows no release from little things.

AMELIA EARHART,
1897-1937, American aviator, writer

The soul is a breath of living spirit,
that with excellent sensitivity,
permeates the entire body
to give it life. Just so, the breath
of the air makes the earth fruitful.
Thus the air is the soul of the earth,
moistening it, greening it.

HILDEGARD OF BINGEN,
1098-1179, German nun, Christian mystic, poet

JANUARY 17

January 18

"Hope" is the thing with feathers—
  That perches in the soul—
And sings the tune without the words—
  And never stops—at all.

EMILY DICKINSON,
1830-1886, American poet

*E*ach one of us is God's special work of art. Through us, He teaches and inspires, delights and encourages, informs and uplifts all those who view our lives. God, the master artist, is most concerned about expressing Himself—His thoughts and His intentions—through what He paints in our character.... [He] wants to paint a beautiful portrait of His Son in and through your life. A painting like no other in all of time.

JONI EARECKSON TADA,
1950- , American writer, speaker

*J*ANUARY 19

January 20

It doesn't take monumental feats to make the world a better place. It can be as simple as letting someone go ahead of you in a grocery line.

BARBARA JOHNSON,
Contemporary, American writer, speaker

You're blessed when you care. At the moment of being "care-full," you find yourselves cared for. You're blessed when you get your inside world—your mind and heart—put right. Then you can see God in the outside world.

MATTHEW 5:7-8 THE MESSAGE

$\mathcal{A}$s parents, we must be convinced of our beliefs. We must know where we stand, so that our children will know where they stand.

KIM BOYCE,
Contemporary, American singer, writer

$\mathcal{J}$ANUARY 21

JANUARY 22

*I*f you believe in a God who controls the big things, you have to believe in a God who controls the little things. It is we, of course, to whom things look "little" or "big."

ELISABETH ELLIOT,
1926- , American writer, m. martyred missionary Jim Elliot

*S*ome people give time,
some money, some their skills
and connections; some literally
give their blood...but everyone
has something to give.

BARBARA BUSH,
1925- , American First Lady

*J*ANUARY 23

JANUARY 24

Whatever my individual desires were to be free, I was not alone. There were many others who felt the same way.

ROSA PARKS,
1913- , American civil rights activist

𝒢od is bigger than any disability.
Love Him, appreciate His
blessings, and trust Him for
the rest of the journey.
He puts the rainbow at the
end of the hardest trail.

DALE EVANS ROGERS,
1912-2001, American actor, m. Roy Rogers

𝒥ANUARY 25

January 26

There must always be a remedy for wrong and injustice if we only know how to find it.

IDA B. WELLS,
1862-1931, African-American journalist and activist

Without God, it is utterly impossible. But with God everything is possible.

MARK 10:27 TLB

*W*hat a strange thing is memory,
and hope; one looks backward,
the other forward. The one is of today,
the other is of tomorrow. Memory
is history recorded in our brain,
memory is a painter, it paints pictures
of the past and of the day.

GRANDMA MOSES (ANNA MARY ROBERTSON)
1860-1961, American artist

*J*ANUARY 27

JANUARY 28

We cannot always understand the ways of Almighty God—the crosses which He sends us, the sacrifices which He demands of us.... But we accept with faith and resignation His holy will with no looking back to what might have been, and we are at peace.

ROSE FITZGERALD KENNEDY,
1890-1995, mother of John F. Kennedy

*W*e live in the present, we dream
of the future, but we learn
eternal truths from the past.

Lucy Maud Montgomery,
1874-1942, Canadian writer

*J*ANUARY 29

JANUARY 30

*A*ction is indeed the sole medium
of expression for ethics.

JANE ADDAMS,
1860-1935, American social reformer, Nobel Prize winner

*Therefore, as we have opportunity,
let us do good to all people.*

GALATIANS 6:10 NIV

[*A*stronomical] observations...
are peculiarly adapted to women....
The eye that directs a needle in the
delicate meshes of embroidery will
equally well bisect a star with the
spider web of the micrometer.

MARIA MITCHELL,
1818-1889, American astronomer, educator

*J*ANUARY 31

FEBRUARY 1

I don't know that there are any short cuts to doing a good job.

SANDRA DAY O'CONNOR,
1930- , American Supreme Court Justice

_ight tomorrow with today!

ELIZABETH BARRETT BROWNING,
1806-1861, British poet

*Faith is being sure of what we hope
for and certain of what we do not see.*

HEBREWS 11:1 NIV

EBRUARY 2

FEBRUARY 3

Peace is not placidity: peace is
The power to endure the
megatron of pain
With joy, the silent thunder of release,
The ordering of Love.
Peace is the atom's start,
The primal image:
God within the heart.

MADELEINE L'ENGLE,
1918- , American writer

*P*ractice means to perform,
over and over again in the face of
all obstacles, some act of vision,
of faith, of desire. Practice is a means
of inviting the perfection desired.

MARTHA GRAHAM,
1894-1991, American dancer, choreographer, educator

*F*EBRUARY 4

FEBRUARY 5

When you get into a tight place and everything goes against you, till it seems as though you could not hang on a minute longer, never give up then, for that is just the place and time that the tide will turn.

HARRIET BEECHER STOWE,
1811-1896, American writer

$\mathcal{T}$he greatness of the human personality begins at the hour of birth. From this almost mystic affirmation there comes what may seem a strange conclusion: that education must start from birth.

MARIA MONTESSORI,
*1870-1952, Italian educator, physician,
originator Montessori Method*

$\mathcal{F}$EBRUARY 6

FEBRUARY 7

*B*elieve in yourself, learn,
and never stop wanting
to build a better world.

MARY McLEOD BETHUNE,
1875-1955, American educator, writer

*Encourage each other to build each other up,
just as you are already doing.*

1 THESSALONIANS 5:11 TLB

*T*his is my letter to the world,
That never wrote to me,
The simple news that Nature told,
With tender majesty.
Her message is committed,
To hands I cannot see;
For love of her, sweet countrymen,
Judge tenderly of me.

EMILY DICKINSON,
1830-1886, American poet

*F*EBRUARY 8

FEBRUARY 9

The wonder of our Lord is that He is
so accessible to us in the common
things of our lives: the cup of
water...breaking of the bread...
welcoming children into our
arms...fellowship over a meal...
giving thanks. A simple attitude
of caring, listening,
and lovingly telling the truth.

NANCIE CARMICHAEL,
Contemporary, American writer, singer/songwriter

God, with all His giving heart,
can only give us Himself
as we recognize the depth
of the need in our own lives.

Eugenia Price,
1916-1996, American writer

FEBRUARY 10

FEBRUARY 11

You gain strength, courage
and confidence by every
experience in which you really
stop to look fear in the face.
You must do the thing you
think you cannot do.

ELEANOR ROOSEVELT,
1884-1962, American First Lady, humanitarian

*N*ever doubt that a small group of thoughtful, committed citizens can change the world. Indeed, it is the only thing that ever has.

MARGARET MEAD,
1901-1978, American anthropologist, writer

Nothing is impossible with God.

LUKE 1:37 NIV

EBRUARY 12

FEBRUARY 13

I am for lifting everyone off
the social bottom. In fact,
I am for doing away with
the social bottom altogether.

CLARE BOOTHE LUCE,
1903- , American diplomat, politician

*W*e learn to believe by believing.
We learn to love by loving.
The practice of acting on
a certain thing, even (or especially)
when feeling is absent, embodies
the entire "how" of growth.

EUGENIA PRICE,
1916-1996, American writer

FEBRUARY 14

FEBRUARY 15

*I*t is the simple things of life
that make living worthwhile,
the sweet fundamental things
such as love and duty, work
and rest, and living close to nature.

LAURA INGALLS WILDER,
1867-1957, *American children's writer*

*Every good and perfect gift is from above,
coming down from the Father of the
heavenly lights, who does not change
like shifting shadows.*

JAMES 1:17 NIV

If all were rain and never sun,
No bow could span the hill;
If all were sun and never rain,
There'd be no rainbow still.

CHRISTINA ROSSETTI,
1830-1894, British poet, lyricist

FEBRUARY 16

FEBRUARY 17

*T*he center of power is not to be found in summit meetings or in peace conferences. It is not in Peking or Washington or the United Nations, but rather where a child of God prays in the power of the Spirit for God's will to be done in her life, in her home, and in the world about her.

RUTH BELL GRAHAM,
1920- , American writer, m. Billy Graham

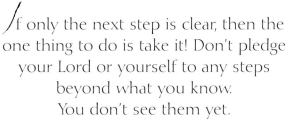

*I*f only the next step is clear, then the one thing to do is take it! Don't pledge your Lord or yourself to any steps beyond what you know. You don't see them yet.

AMY CARMICHAEL,
1867-1951, Irish missionary to India, poet

FEBRUARY 18

FEBRUARY 19

It is never enough to know about spiritual things with your mind. Mental knowledge is not the same thing as truly understanding from the center of your being, which results from experiencing and doing.

TERESA OF AVILA,
1515-1582, Spanish Christian mystic, writer

When one door of happiness closes,
another opens; but often we look
so long at the closed door that
we do not see the one which
has been opened for us.

HELEN KELLER,
1919-1985, American writer, crusader for the handicapped

"For I know the plans I have for you,"
declares the Lord, "plans to prosper
you and not to harm you, plans
to give you hope and a future."

JEREMIAH 29:11 NIV

EBRUARY 20

FEBRUARY 21

$\mathcal{T}$he measure of a life, after all, is not
its duration but its donation.

CORRIE TEN BOOM,
1892-1983, Dutch evangelist, writer

*N*o one can arrive from being
talented alone. God gives talent,
work transforms talent into genius.

Anna Pavlova,
1881-1931, Russian ballerina

FEBRUARY 22

FEBRUARY 23

*E*ternity is not something that
begins after you are dead. It is going
on all the time. We are in it now.

CHARLOTTE PERKINS GILMAN,
1860-1935, American writer, social critic

$\mathcal{T}$o love God, to serve Him because
we love Him, is...our highest
happiness. Love makes all labor light.
We serve with enthusiasm
where we love with sincerity.

HANNAH MORE,
1745-1833, British writer, social reformer

$\mathcal{F}$EBRUARY 24

FEBRUARY 25

*B*lues are the songs of despair, but gospel songs are the songs of hope.

MAHALIA JACKSON,
1911-1972, American gospel singer

May the God of hope fill you with all joy and peace in believing, so that you may abound in hope.

ROMANS 15:13 NIV

*A*lways stay connected to people and seek out things that bring you joy. Dream with abandon. Pray confidently.

BARBARA JOHNSON,
Contemporary, American writer, speaker

FEBRUARY 26

FEBRUARY 27

There isn't a man or a woman
anywhere, I am convinced,
who does not long for tenderness.

ELISABETH ELLIOT,
1926- , American writer,
m. martyred missionary Jim Elliot

*B*efore anything else, above all else,
beyond everything else, God loves us.
God loves us extravagantly,
ridiculously, without limit
or condition. God is in love
with us…God yearns for us.

ROBERTA BONDI,
Contemporary, American educator, writer

*F*EBRUARY 28

FEBRUARY 29

*W*omen, if the soul of the nation
is to be saved, I believe that
you must become its soul.

CORETTA SCOTT KING,
1927- , American civil rights activist, writer

*D*o what you can to show you care
about other people, and you will
make our world a better place.

ROSALYNN CARTER,
1927- , American First Lady

Love others as you love yourself.
That's an act of true freedom.

GALATIANS 5:14 THE MESSAGE

*M*ARCH 1

MARCH 2

For me it's the challenge—
the challenge to try to beat myself
or do better than I did in the past.
I try to keep in mind not what
I have accomplished but what I have
to try to accomplish in the future.

JACKIE JOYNER KERSEE,
1962- , American Olympic gold medalist

*T*he story of a love is not
important—what is important
is that one is capable of love.
It is perhaps the only glimpse
we are permitted of eternity.

HELEN HAYES,
1900-1993, American actor

*M*ARCH 3

MARCH 4

I have suffered a lot from both physical and emotional pain. Sometimes I thought I could not live, but God saved me and gave me faith and hope.

KIM PHUC,
1963- , Vietnam War survivor of Napalm bomb

*W*e may run, walk, stumble, drive, or fly, but let us never lose sight of the reason for the journey, or miss a chance to see a rainbow on the way.

GLORIA GAITHER,
Contemporary, American writer, singer/songwriter

MARCH 5

MARCH 6

In every outthrust headland, in every curving beach, in every grain of sand there is a story of the earth.

RACHEL CARSON,
1907-1964, American biologist, writer

What a wildly wonderful world, God! You made it all, with Wisdom at your side, made earth overflow with your wonderful creations.

PSALM 104:24 THE MESSAGE

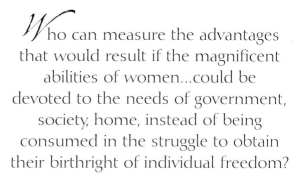

*W*ho can measure the advantages that would result if the magnificent abilities of women...could be devoted to the needs of government, society, home, instead of being consumed in the struggle to obtain their birthright of individual freedom?

Susan B. Anthony,
1820-1906, American suffragist

*M*arch 7

MARCH 8

Just opening up the door,
having this ordinary person fly,
says a lot for the future. You can
always equate astronauts with
explorers who were subsidized.
Now you are getting someone
going just to observe.
And then you'll have the settlers.

CHRISTA MCAULIFFE,
1948-1986, American educator,
member of space shuttle Challenger

Heavenly Father, speak to me today concerning how to reach out to the world. From the youngest to the oldest, there is something we all can do.

KIM BOYCE,
Contemporary, American singer, writer

MARCH 9

MARCH 10

We hold these truths to be
self-evident: that all men
and women are created equal.

ELIZABETH CADY STANTON,
1815-1902, American suffragist, social reformer

*N*o matter what the circumstances are, it is best to pursue behavior that is above reproach, because then you will be respected for your actions.

Rosa Parks,
1913- , American civil rights activist

Be content with who you are, and don't put on airs. God's strong hand is on you; he'll promote you at the right time. Live carefree before God; he is most careful with you.

1 Peter 5:6-7 the Message

*M*arch 11

MARCH 12

You cannot hope to build
a better world without improving
the individuals. To that end each
of us must work for her own
improvement, and at the same
time share a general responsibility
for all humanity, our particular
duty being to aid those to whom
we think we can be most useful.

MARIE CURIE,
1867-1934, Polish-born French physicist

*O*ur feelings do not affect God's facts. They may blow up, like clouds, and cover the eternal things that we do most truly believe. We may not see the shining of the promises—but they still shine! [His strength] is not for one moment less because of our human weakness.

AMY CARMICHAEL,
1867-1951, Irish missionary to India, poet

*M*ARCH 13

*M*ARCH 14

*P*rayer unites the soul to God, for
although the soul may always be like
God in nature and substance, it is
often unlike Him in condition.

JULIAN OF NORWICH,
1342-1413, British Christian mystic

I am not writing just for the sake of writing. I have attempted to convey...a message, which God has given, and to convey that message with whatever abilities were given to me. Whatever I've been able to accomplish has been God's doing. I've tried to follow His teachings in all my writing and thoughts.

GRACE LIVINGSTON HILL,
1865-1947, American writer

*M*ARCH 15

MARCH 16

$\mathscr{G}$ood communication is as
stimulating as black coffee,
and just as hard to sleep after.

ANNE MORROW LINDBERGH,
1906-2001, American writer; m. Charles Lindbergh

*I*n spite of everything I still believe
that people are really good at heart.
I simply can't build up my hopes
on a foundation consisting
of confusion, misery and death.

ANNE FRANK,
1929-1945, German Jewish diarist

*M*ARCH 17

MARCH 18

The secret of joy in work is
contained in one word—excellence.
To know how to do something
well is to enjoy it.

PEARL S. BUCK,
1892-1973, American writer, Nobel Prize winner

*In everything you do, put God first,
and he will direct you and crown
your efforts with success.*

PROVERBS 3:6 TLB

I have learned from experience that the greater part of our happiness or misery depends on our dispositions and not on our circumstances.

MARTHA WASHINGTON,
1732-1802, American First Lady

*M*ARCH 19

MARCH 20

With each new experience of letting God be in control, we gain courage and reinforcement for daring to do it again and again.

GLORIA GAITHER,
Contemporary, American writer, singer/songwriter

Make the least of all that goes and the most of all that comes. Don't regret what is past. Cherish what you have. Look forward to all that is to come. And most important of all, rely moment by moment on Jesus.

GIGI GRAHAM TCHIVIDJIAN,
1945- , American writer, speaker, d. Billy Graham

MARCH 21

MARCH 22

Nothing great was ever done without much enduring.

CATHERINE OF SIENA,
1347-1380, Italian Christian mystic

My…sisters, whenever you face trials of any kind, consider it nothing but joy…and let endurance have its full effect, so that you may be mature and complete, lacking in nothing.

JAMES 1:2,4 NRSV

*W*e must not, in trying to think about how we can make a big difference, ignore the small daily differences we can make which, over time, add up to big differences that we often cannot foresee.

MARION WRIGHT EDELMAN,
1937- , American attorney, civil rights activist

MARCH 23

MARCH 24

With God, life is eternal—both in quality and length. There is no joy comparable to the joy of discovering something new from God, about God. If the continuing life is a life of joy, we will go on discovering, learning.

EUGENIA PRICE,
1916-1996, *American writer*

_I_t is God to whom and with
whom we travel, and while
He is the End of our journey,
He is also at every stopping place.

ELISABETH ELLIOT,
1926-, American writer,
m. martyred missionary Jim Elliot

_M_ARCH 25

MARCH 26

The Lord's chief desire is to reveal
Himself to you and, in order for Him
to do that, He gives you abundant
grace. The Lord gives you the
experience of enjoying His presence.
He touches you, and His touch
is so delightful that, more than ever,
you are drawn inwardly to Him.

MADAME JEANNE GUYON,
1648-1717, French Christian mystic

*O*bstacles are those frightful
things you see when you
take your eyes off the goal.

HANNAH MORE,
1745-1833, British writer, social reformer

*Don't worry about anything; instead, pray
about everything; tell God your needs
and...thank him for his answers.*

PHILIPPIANS 4:6-7 TLB

*M*ARCH 27

MARCH 28

Love is the divine vitality that
everywhere produces
and restores life. To each
and every one of us,
it gives the power of working
miracles if we will.

LYDIA MARIE CHILD,
1802-1880, American abolitionist, writer

It is not how many years
we live, but what
we do with them.

Catherine Booth,
*1829-1890, British evangelist,
first woman Salvation Army general*

March 29

MARCH 30

God's way of dealing with us [is] to throw us into situations over our depth, then supply us with the necessary ability to swim.

CATHERINE MARSHALL,
1914-1983, American writer

*I*ntricately woven, a blanket of stars
covers the night sky, each star set in
its place, reflecting its perfect light.
All the stars together make a grand
display, glimmering and shimmering
in a unique expression of praise
to the Creator of them all.

WENDY MOORE,
1971- , American writer

*M*ARCH 31

APRIL 1

Never be afraid to trust an unknown future to an all-knowing God.

CORRIE TEN BOOM,
1892-1983, Dutch evangelist, writer

*N*o trumpets sound when
the important decisions
of our life are made.
Destiny is made known silently.

AGNES DeMILLE,
1905- , American dancer, choreographer

*A*PRIL 2

APRIL 3

To put yourself in another's place requires real imagination, but by so doing each Girl Scout will be able to live among others happily.

JULIETTE LOW,
1860-1927, British/American humanitarian,
founder of Girl Scouts of America

*E*veryone has inside herself a piece
of good news! The good news is that
you really don't know how great
you can be, how much you can love,
what you can accomplish
and what your potential is.

ANNE FRANK,
1929-1945, German Jewish diarist

*Isn't everything you have and everything
you are sheer gifts from God?...
You already have all you need.*

1 CORINTHIANS 4:7-8 THE MESSAGE

*A*PRIL 4

*S*pend all you have for loveliness,
Buy it and never count the cost;
For one white singing hour of peace
Count many a year of strife well lost,
And for a breath of ecstasy
Give all you have been, or could be.

SARA TEASDALE,
1884-1933, American poet

Spring bursts today,
For love is risen and all
the earth's at play.

CHRISTINA ROSSETTI,
1830-1894, British poet, lyricist

APRIL 6

APRIL 7

We are of such value to God that He came to live among us...and to guide us home. He will go to any length to seek us, even to being lifted high upon the cross to draw us back to Himself. We can only respond by loving God for His love.

CATHERINE OF SIENA,
1347-1380, Italian Christian mystic

$\mathcal{O}$ne can get just as much
exultation in losing oneself
in a little thing as in a big thing.
It is nice to think how one can be
recklessly lost in a daisy!

ANNE MORROW LINDBERGH,
1906-2001, American writer, m. Charles Lindbergh

$\mathcal{A}$PRIL 8

APRIL 9

Leadership should be born out of the understanding of the needs of those who would be affected by it.

MARIAN ANDERSON,
1902-1993, American singer

*A wise person gets known for insight;
gracious words add to one's reputation.*

PROVERBS 16:21 THE MESSAGE

The human heart,
   has hidden treasures,
In secret kept, in silence sealed; —
The thoughts, the hopes, the dreams,
   the pleasures,
Whose charms were broken
   if revealed.

CHARLOTTE BRONTË,
1816-1855, British writer

*A*PRIL 10

APRIL 11

I am convinced beyond a shadow of any doubt that the most valuable pursuit we can embark upon is to know God.

KAY ARTHUR,
1933- , American writer

$\mathcal{G}$od wears Himself out through the infinite thickness of time and space in order to reach the soul and to captivate it.... The soul, starting from the opposite end, makes the same journey that God made towards it. And that is the cross.

SIMONE WEIL,
1910-1943, French revolutionary, philosopher

$\mathcal{A}$PRIL 12

APRIL 13

*M*odern invention has banished
the spinning-wheel, and the same
law of progress makes the woman
of today a different woman
from her grandmother.

SUSAN B. ANTHONY,
1820-1906, American suffragist

*H*elping one another is part of the
religion of our sisterhood.

LOUISA MAY ALCOTT,
1832-1888, American writer

*May God who gives patience, steadiness, and
encouragement help you to live in complete
harmony with each other.*

ROMANS 15:5 TLB

*A*PRIL 14

April 15

*I*t is easier to gaze into the sun,
than into the face
of the mystery of God.
Such is its beauty and its radiance.

HILDEGARD OF BINGEN,
1098-1179, German nun, Christian mystic, poet

*T*here is nothing like staying
at home for real comfort.

JANE AUSTEN,
1775-1817, British writer

*A*PRIL 16

APRIL 17

Hold fast your dreams!
Within your heart
Keep one still, secret spot
Where dreams may go
And, sheltered so,
May thrive and grow
Where doubt and fear are not.
O keep a place apart,
Within your heart,
For little dreams to go!

LOUISE DRISCOLL,
1875-1957, American poet, writer

*T*here may be no trumpet sound
or loud applause when we make
a right decision, just a calm sense
of resolution and peace.

GLORIA GAITHER,
Contemporary, American writer, singer/songwriter

*A*PRIL 18

April 19

*T*ruth does not change according to our ability to stomach it emotionally.

FLANNERY O'CONNOR,
1925-1964, American writer

Don't become so well-adjusted to your culture that you fit into it without even thinking. Instead, fix your attention on God. You'll be changed from the inside out.... Unlike the culture around you, always dragging you down to its level of immaturity, God brings the best out of you, develops well-formed maturity in you.

ROMANS 12:2 THE MESSAGE

*W*hen indeed shall we learn that we are all related one to the other, that we are all members of one body? Until the spirit of love for our fellow man, regardless of race, color or creed, shall fill the world, making real in our lives and our deeds the actuality of human brotherhood— until the great mass of the people shall be filled with the sense of responsibility for each other's welfare, social justice can never be attained.

HELEN KELLER,
1919-1985, American writer, crusader for the handicapped

*A*PRIL 20

APRIL 21

The God of the universe—the One who created everything and holds it all in His hand—created each of us in His image, to bear His likeness, His imprint. It is only when Christ dwells within our hearts, radiating the pure light of His love through our humanity, that we discover who we are and what we were intended to be. There is no other joy that reaches as deep or as wide or as high—there is no other joy that is more complete.

WENDY MOORE,
1971- , American writer

I don't think there is anyone who needs God's help and grace as much as I do. Sometimes I feel so helpless and weak. I think that is why God uses me. Because I cannot depend on my own strength, I rely on Him twenty-four hours a day.

MOTHER TERESA OF CALCUTTA,
1910-1997, Roman Catholic nun, Nobel Peace Prize winner

*A*PRIL 22

April 23

I do not know anyone who has got to the top without hard work. That is the recipe. It will not always get you to the top, but it should get you pretty near.

MARGARET THATCHER,
1925- , former Prime Minister of Great Britain

*T*he woman who creates and sustains a home, and under whose hands children grow up to be strong and pure men and women, is a creator second only to God.

HELEN HUNT JACKSON,
1830-1855, American writer, Indian rights reformer

And God is able to make all grace abound to you, so that in all things at all times, having all that you need, you will abound in every good work.

2 CORINTHIANS 9:8 NIV

*A*PRIL 24

April 25

Far rather would I sit and sew beside my poor mother, for this thing is not of my condition. But I must go, and I must do this thing, because my Lord will have it so. Rather now than tomorrow, and tomorrow than the day after!

JOAN OF ARC,
1412-1431, French patriot and martyr

By putting the gift of yearning for God into every human being's heart, God at the same time draws all people made in God's image to God's self and into their own true selves.

ROBERTA BONDI,
Contemporary, American educator, writer

April 26

April 27

The very act of planting a seed
in the earth has in it to me something
beautiful. I always do it with a joy
that is largely mixed with awe.

CELIA LAIGHTON THAXTER,
1835-1894, American poet

Love the moment. Flowers grow out of dark moments. Therefore, each moment is vital. It affects the whole. Life is a succession of such moments and to live each is to succeed.

CORITA KENT,
1918-1986, American artist

*A*PRIL 28

_A_PRIL 29

_A_ good laugh is as good
as a prayer sometimes.

LUCY MAUD MONTGOMERY,
1874-1942, Canadian writer

She is clothed with strength and dignity;
she can laugh at the days to come.

PROVERBS 31:25 NIV

_Y_outh is, after all, just a moment,
but it is the moment,
the spark that you always
carry in your heart.

RAISA GORBACHEV,
1932- , Russian, USSR First Lady

_A_PRIL 30

$\mathcal{M}$AY 1

$\mathcal{T}$he God who created, names, and
numbers the stars in the heavens also
numbers the hairs of my head....
He pays attention to very big
things and to very small ones.
What matters to me matters to Him,
and that changes my life.

ELISABETH ELLIOT,
1926- , American writer, m. martyred missionary Jim Elliot

*I*f you are unhappy with your lot in
life, build a service station on it.

CORRIE TEN BOOM,
1892-1983, Dutch evangelist, writer

*M*AY 2

MAY 3

I am a big believer that you have to nourish any relationship. I am still very much a part of my friends' lives and they are very much a part of my life.

NANCY REAGAN,
1923- , American First Lady, actor

*T*he most practical thing
in the world is common sense
and common humanity.

LADY NANCY ASTOR,
1879-1964, British, first woman Member of Parliament

Dear friend, guard Clear Thinking
and Common Sense with your life;
don't for a minute lose sight of them.
They'll keep your soul alive and well,
they'll keep you fit and attractive.

PROVERBS 3:21-22 THE MESSAGE

*M*AY 4

*M*AY 5

*T*hose who contemplate the beauty
of the earth find reserves of strength
that will endure as long as life lasts.
There is symbolic as well as actual
beauty in the migration of the birds,
the ebb and flow of the tides, the
folded bud ready for the spring. There
is something infinitely healing in the
repeated refrains of nature—the
assurance that dawn comes after
night, and spring after the winter.

RACHEL CARSON,
1907-1964, American biologist, writer

*W*e are so busy in our lives that
we need to purposely give attention
to the everyday things that can make
our lives lovelier, such as keeping a
vase of fresh flowers in an obvious
place, or several places in the house.
Planting roses or other flowers
for this purpose makes sense.

EMILIE BARNES,
1938- , American speaker, writer

*M*AY 6

MAY 7

Let every woman become so cultivated and refined in intellect, that her taste and judgment will be respected...so unassuming and unambitious, that collision and competition will be banished...then, the fathers, the husbands, and the sons, will find an influence thrown around them, to which they will yield not only willingly but proudly.

CATHERINE BEECHER,
1800-1878, American educator

*T*he splendor of the rose and the whiteness of the lily do not rob the little violet of its scent nor the daisy of its simple charm. If every tiny flower wanted to be a rose, spring would lose its loveliness.

THÉRÈSE OF LISIEUX,
1873-1897, French Carmelite nun

*M*AY 8

$\mathcal{M}$ AY 9

$\mathcal{M}$ ay your life become one of glad
and unending praise to the Lord as
you journey through this world, and
in the world that is to come!

TERESA OF AVILA,
1515-1582, Spanish Christian mystic, writer

You've always been great toward me—
what love!... You, O God,
are both tender and kind, not easily angered,
immense in love, and you never, never quit.

PSALM 86:13,15 THE MESSAGE

$\mathcal{F}$or whatever life holds
for you and your family
in the coming days, weave
the unfailing fabric of God's Word
through your heart and mind.
It will hold strong, even
if the rest of life unravels.

GIGI GRAHAM TCHIVIDJIAN,
1945- , American writer, speaker, d. Billy Graham

$\mathcal{M}$AY 10

$\mathcal{M}$AY 11

$\mathcal{W}$e plant seeds that will flower
as results in our lives, so best to
remove the weeds of anger, avarice,
envy and doubt, that peace and
abundance may manifest for all.

DOROTHY DAY,
1897-1980, American writer, social reformer

*I*f I'm not free to fail, I'm not free to take risks, and everything in life that's worth doing involves a willingness to take a risk and involves the risk of failure.... I have to try, but I do not have to succeed.

MADELEINE L'ENGLE,
1918- , American writer

*M*AY 12

MAY 13

In a world where there is so much to be done, I felt strongly impressed that there must be something for me to do.

DOROTHEA DIX,
1802-1887, American humanitarian and reformer

$\mathcal{T}$he beauty of a woman is not
in the clothes she wears,
The figure that she carries, or the way
she combs her hair.
The beauty of a woman must be seen
from in her eyes,
Because that is the doorway to her heart
the place where love resides.

AUDREY HEPBURN,
1929-1993, Belgian actor

*Cultivate inner beauty, the gentle,
gracious kind that God delights in.*

1 PETER 3:4 THE MESSAGE

$\mathcal{M}$AY 14

MAY 15

You find yourself refreshed by the presence of cheerful people. Why not make an honest effort to confer that pleasure on others? Half the battle is gained if you never allow yourself to say anything gloomy.

LYDIA MARIE CHILD,
1802-1880, *American abolitionist, writer*

*G*iving encouragement to others
is a most welcome gift, for the results
of it are lifted spirits, increased
self-worth, and a hopeful future.

FLORENCE LITTAUER,
1928- , American speaker, writer

*M*AY 16

MAY 17

*B*ecause I have a heart for God I also have a heart for women. As I hear their stories, I realize so many feel themselves to be inadequate. What a joy it is to believe them into doing those things they never believed they could do and being the people they never believed they could be.

JILL BRISCOE,
1935- , American speaker, writer

*L*ove is extravagant in the price
it is willing to pay, the time it is willing
to give, the hardships it is willing
to endure, and the strength it is
willing to spend. Love never thinks
in terms of "how little," but always
in terms of "how much." Love gives,
love knows, and love lasts.

JONI EARECKSON TADA,
1950- , American writer, speaker

*M*AY 18

MAY 19

*T*hat it will never come again is what
makes life so sweet.

EMILY DICKINSON,
1830-1886, American poet

Pursue a righteous life—a life of wonder,
faith, love, steadiness, courtesy. Run hard
and fast in the faith. Seize the eternal life,
the life you were called to.

1 TIMOTHY 6:11-12 THE MESSAGE

Love works in ways that
are wondrous and strange,
There is nothing in life that
Love cannot change.

HELEN STEINER RICE,
1900-1981, American poet

MAY 20

MAY 21

God delights to meet the faith
of one who looks up to Him and says,
"Lord, You know that I cannot do
this—but I believe that You can!"

AMY CARMICHAEL,
1867-1951, Irish missionary to India, poet

$\mathcal{A}$t the end of your life you will
never regret not having passed one
more test, not winning one more
verdict, or not closing one more deal.
You will regret time not spent with a
husband, a friend, a child, or a parent.

BARBARA BUSH,
1925- , American First Lady

$\mathcal{M}$AY 22

MAY 23

*S*uccess can make you go one
of two ways. It can make you
a prima donna—or it can smooth
the edges, take away the insecurities,
let the nice things come out.

BARBARA WALTERS,
1931- , American broadcast journalist

God is everything that is good and comfortable for us. He is our clothing that for love wraps us, clasps us, and all surrounds us for tender love.

Julian of Norwich,
1342-1413, British Christian mystic

For God is sheer beauty, all-generous in love, loyal always and ever.

Psalm 100:5 the message

May 24

MAY 25

*W*omen observe subconsciously
a thousand little details, without
knowing they are doing so.
Their subconscious mind adds
these little things together—
and they call the result intuition.

AGATHA CHRISTIE,
1891-1975, British mystery writer, playwright

*T*he things that matter the most
in this world, they can never
be held in our hand.

GLORIA GAITHER,
Contemporary, American writer, singer/songwriter

*M*AY 26

MAY 27

$\mathcal{G}$od looks at the world through
the eyes of love. If we, therefore,
as human beings made in the image
of God also want to see reality
rationally, that is, as it truly is,
then we, too, must learn to look
at what we see with love.

ROBERTA BONDI,
Contemporary, American educator, writer

If we would build on a sure foundation in friendship we must love friends for their sake rather than our own.

CHARLOTTE BRONTË,
1816-1855, British writer

*M*AY 28

*M*AY 29

*S*howing kindness to others
is one of the nicest things
we can do for ourselves.

JANETTE OKE,
1935- , American writer

He who refreshes others will
himself be refreshed.

PROVERBS 11:25 NIV

*I*n spite of the cost of living,
it's still popular.

KATHLEEN NORRIS,
1947- , American writer

*M*AY 30

MAY 31

*A*fter the verb "To Love"...
"To Help" is the most beautiful
verb in the world.

BERTHA VON SUTTNER,
1843-1914, writer, Nobel Peace Prize winner

*O*h better than the minting
Of a gold-crowned king
Is the safe-kept memory
Of a lovely thing.

*May the Lord continually
bless you with heaven's blessings
as well as with human joys.*

*J*UNE 1

JUNE 2

We can never untangle all the
woes in other people's lives.
We can't produce miracles overnight.
But we can bring a cup of cool
water to a thirsty soul, or a scoop
of laughter to a lonely heart.

BARBARA JOHNSON,
Contemporary, American writer, speaker

O the pure delight of a single hour
That before Thy throne I spend,
When I kneel in prayer,
    and with Thee, my God,
I commune as friend with friend!

FANNY CROSBY,
1820-1915, hymn writer

*J*UNE 3

JUNE 4

A little praise is not only
merest justice but is beyond
the purse of no one.

EMILY POST,
1873-1960, American writer, socialite

*I*n today's world...it is still women's business to make life better, to make tomorrow better than today.

HELEN THAMES RALEY,
1909- , American writer

*J*UNE 5

JUNE 6

*I*nvest in the human soul.
Who knows, it might be
a diamond in the rough.

MARY McLEOD BETHUNE,
1875-1955, American educator, writer

*Give generously, for your gifts
will return to you later.*

ECCLESIASTES 11:1 TLB

The great thing about getting older is that you don't lose all the other ages you've been.

MADELEINE L'ENGLE,
1918- , American writer

JUNE 7

JUNE 8

*I*f you don't like the way
the world is, you change it.
You have an obligation to change it.
You just do it one step at a time.

MARION WRIGHT EDELMAN,
1937- , American attorney, civil rights activist

*G*od has not promised skies always blue,
flower-strewn pathways all our lives through;
God has not promised sun without rain,
joy without sorrow, peace without pain.
But God has promised strength for the day,
rest for the labor, light for the way,
grace for the trials, help from above,
unfailing sympathy, undying love.

ANNIE JOHNSON FLINT,
1866-1932, American poet

*J*UNE 9

JUNE 10

*B*ig doesn't necessarily mean better. Sunflowers aren't better than violets.

EDNA FERBER,
1887-1968, American writer

*T*he basic experience of everyone is
the experience of human limitation.

FLANNERY O'CONNOR,
1925-1964, *American writer*

*Don't lose a minute in building on what
you've been given, complementing your
basic faith with good character, spiritual
understanding, alert discipline, passionate
patience, reverent wonder, warm friendliness,
and generous love, each dimension fitting
into and developing the others.*

2 PETER 1:5 THE MESSAGE

*J*UNE 11

JUNE 12

Take your work seriously,
but never yourself.

DAME MARGOT FONTEYN,
1919-1991, British ballerina

*H*eavenly Father,
Teach me not to procrastinate but
to do what I can today, because there
is no promise of tomorrow. Lead me
to those people who are in need
of something that I can give. I want
to be available for You to use in any
way that You should choose. Amen.

KIM BOYCE,
Contemporary, American singer, writer

*J*UNE 13

JUNE 14

In a special way, human beings…being made in the image of God, only become real human beings, are only able to grow and thrive as human beings as they also yearn for God.

ROBERTA BONDI,
Contemporary, American educator, writer

*W*e have a hunger of the mind
which asks for knowledge of all
around us; and the more we gain,
the more is our desire.
The more we see, the more
we are capable of seeing.

MARIA MITCHELL,
1818-1889, American astronomer, educator

*J*UNE 15

JUNE 16

$/$he one thing that doesn't abide by
majority rule is a person's conscience.

HARPER LEE,
1926- , American writer, Pulitzer Prize winner

*Let love and faithfulness never leave
you...write them on the tablet of your heart.*

PROVERBS 3:3 NIV

*E*ven if your efforts seem for years
to be producing no result, one day
a light that is in exact proportion
to them will flood your soul.

SIMONE WEIL,
1910-1943, French revolutionary, philosopher

*J*UNE 17

JUNE 18

Often God has to shut a door
in our face, so that He can
subsequently open the door through
which He wants us to go.

CATHERINE MARSHALL,
1914-1983, American writer

A ship in port is safe, but that is not what ships are for. Sail out to sea and do new things.

GRACE HOPPER,
1906-1992, American computer programmer

JUNE 19

JUNE 20

A painting [is] a symbol for
the universe. Inside it, each
piece relates to the other. Each
piece is only answerable
to the rest of that little world.
So, probably in the total universe,
there is that kind of total harmony,
but we get only little tastes of it.

CORITA KENT,
1918-1986, American artist

*W*e do not need to search for heaven, over here or over there, in order to find our eternal Father. In fact, we do not even need to speak out loud, for though we speak in the smallest whisper or the most fleeting thought, He is close enough to hear us.

Teresa of Avila,
1515-1582, Spanish Christian mystic, writer

*The Lord…is close to all who
call on him sincerely.*

Psalm 145:17-18 tlb

*J*une 21

JUNE 22

I believe the second half of one's
life is meant to be better than
the first half. The first half
is finding out how you do it.
And the second half is enjoying it.

FRANCIS LEAR,
1923- , American businesswoman, publisher

*I*f we just give God the little
that we have, we can trust
Him to make it go around.

GLORIA GAITHER,
Contemporary, American writer, singer/songwriter

*J*UNE 23

JUNE 24

I am not afraid of storms for I am
learning how to sail my ship.

LOUISA MAY ALCOTT,
1832-1888, American writer

*W*hat a circus we women
perform every day of our lives.
It puts a trapeze artist to shame.

ANNE MORROW LINDBERGH,
1906-2001, American writer; m. Charles Lindbergh

*J*UNE 25

JUNE 26

*Because of their age-long training
in human relations—for that
is what feminine intuition really is—
women have a special contribution
to make to any group enterprise.*

MARGARET MEAD,
1901-1978, *American anthropologist, writer*

*She speaks with wisdom,
and faithful instruction is on her tongue.*

PROVERBS 31:26 NIV

$\mathcal{G}$od is not in the vastness
of greatness. He is hid
in the vastness of smallness.
He is not in the general.
He is in the particular.

PEARL S. BUCK,
1892-1973, American writer, Nobel Prize winner

$\mathcal{J}$UNE 27

June 28

*W*holehearted, ready laughter heals, encourages, relaxes anyone within hearing distance. The laughter that springs from love makes wide the space around it—gives room for the loved one to enter in. Real laughter welcomes, and never shuts out.

EUGENIA PRICE,
1916-1996, American writer

*F*or as the body is clad in the cloth,
and the flesh in the skin,
and the bones in the flesh,
and the heart in the whole,
so are we, soul and body, clad in the
Goodness of God, and enclosed.

JULIAN OF NORWICH,
1342-1413, British Christian mystic

JUNE 30

Happy people…enjoy the fundamental, often very simple things of life…. They savor the moment, glad to be alive, enjoying their work, their families, the good things around them. They are adaptable; they can bend with the wind, adjust to the changes in their times, enjoy the contest of life…. Their eyes are turned outward; they are aware, compassionate. They have the capacity to love.

JANE CANFIELD,
Contemporary, American writer

*W*hat God gives in answer
to our prayers will always be
the thing we most urgently need,
and it will always be sufficient.

ELISABETH ELLIOT,
1926- , American writer, m. martyred missionary Jim Elliot

*J*ULY 1

July 2

Like billowing clouds, like the
incessant gurgle of the brook,
the longing of the soul can never
be stilled. It is this longing
with which holy persons seek
their work from God.

HILDEGARD OF BINGEN,
1098-1179, German nun, Christian mystic, poet

Life is what we make it, always has been, always will be.

GRANDMA MOSES (*Anna Mary Robertson*)
1860-1961, American artist

What happens when we live God's way?
He brings gifts into our lives…things like
affection for others, exuberance about life,
serenity. We develop a willingness to stick
with things, a sense of compassion
in the heart, and a conviction that a basic
holiness permeates things and people.

GALATIANS 5:22-23 THE MESSAGE

JULY 3

July 4

Isn't it splendid to think of all the
things there are to find out about?
It just makes me feel glad to be
alive—it's such an interesting world.
It wouldn't be half so interesting
if we knew all about everything.

LUCY MAUD MONTGOMERY,
1874-1942, Canadian writer

Every formula which
expresses a law of nature
is a hymn of praise to God.

MARIA MITCHELL,
1818-1889, American astronomer, educator

JULY 5

JULY 6

I cannot count the number of times I have been strengthened by another woman's heartfelt hug, appreciative note, surprise gift, or caring questions.... My friends are an oasis to me, encouraging me to go on. They are essential to my well-being.

DEE BRESTIN,
Contemporary, American writer

You cannot make yourself feel
something you do not feel,
but you can make yourself
do right in spite of your feelings.

PEARL S. BUCK,
1892-1973, American writer, Nobel Prize winner

JULY 7

July 8

Prayer is the way to open ourselves
to God, and the way in which He
shows us our unstable hearts and
begins to strengthen them.

TERESA OF AVILA,
1515-1582, Spanish Christian mystic, writer

God's peace...is far more wonderful
than the human mind can understand.
His peace will keep your thoughts
and your hearts quiet and at rest.

PHILIPPIANS 4:7 TLB

We all live with the objective
of being happy; our lives are
all different and yet the same.

ANNE FRANK,
1929-1945, German Jewish diarist

JULY 9

$\int$ ULY 10

Only in growth, reform,
and change, paradoxically enough,
is true security to be found.

ANNE MORROW LINDBERGH,
1906-2001, American writer; m. Charles Lindbergh

$\mathcal{G}$oals are access lines to the future.
They allow us to run the race
with the finish line firmly established.

EMILIE BARNES,
Contemporary, American writer

$\mathcal{J}$ULY 11

$\mathcal{J}$ULY 12

$\mathcal{C}$ourage...is when you know
you're licked before you begin but
you begin anyway and you see
it through no matter what.

HARPER LEE,
1926- , American writer, Pulitzer Prize winner

*Do not withhold good from those who
deserve it, when it is in your power to act.*

PROVERBS 3:27 NIV

'Twant me, 'twas the Lord.
I always told Him, "I trust in You.
I don't know where to go or what
to do, but I expect You
to lead me," and He always did.

HARRIET TUBMAN,
1820-1913, American abolitionist

July 13

$\int$ULY 14

If it can be verified, we don't need
faith.... Faith is for that which lies
on the other side of reason.
Faith is what makes life bearable,
with all its tragedies and ambiguities
and sudden, startling joys.

MADELEINE L'ENGLE,
1918- , American writer

*E*very day we live is a priceless gift of God, loaded with possibilities to learn something new, to gain fresh insights.

DALE EVANS ROGERS,
1912-2001, American actor, m. Roy Rogers

JULY 15

JULY 16

Failure is just another way to learn
how to do something right.

MARION WRIGHT EDELMAN,
1937- , American attorney, civil rights activist

Love has its source in God, for love is the very essence of His being.

KAY ARTHUR,
1933- , American writer

God's love...is ever and always, eternally present.

PSALM 103:17 THE MESSAGE

*J*ULY 17

JULY 18

A happy woman is one who has no cares at all; a cheerful woman is one who has cares but doesn't let them get her down.

BEVERLY SILLS,
1929- , American opera singer

*W*e rely upon the poets, the philosophers, and the playwrights to articulate what most of us can only feel, in joy or sorrow. They illuminate the thoughts for which we only grope; they give us the strength and balm we cannot find in ourselves. Whenever I feel my courage wavering I rush to them. They give me the wisdom of acceptance, the will and resilience to push on.

HELEN HAYES,
1900-1993, American actor

*J*ULY 19

July 20

For God is, indeed, a wonderful Father who longs to pour out His mercy upon us, and whose majesty is so great that He can transform us from deep within.

TERESA OF AVILA,
1515-1582, Spanish Christian mystic, writer

*T*o love what you do and feel
that it matters—how could
anything be more fun?

KATHARINE GRAHAM,
1917- , American newspaper publisher

JULY 21

JULY 22

*N*othing in life is to be feared.
It is only to be understood.

MARIE CURIE,
1867-1934, Polish-born French physicist

*O the depth of the riches and wisdom
and knowledge of God!*

ROMANS 11:33 NRSV

*C*ivilization is a method
of living, an attitude of equal
respect for all men.

JANE ADDAMS,
1860-1935, American social reformer, Nobel Prize winner

*J*ULY 23

July 24

If we had no winter, the spring would not be so pleasant; if we did not sometimes taste of adversity, prosperity would not be so welcome.

ANNE BRADSTREET,
1612-1672, American writer

*O*pen wide the windows of our spirits and fill us full of light; open wide the door of our hearts, that we may receive and entertain Thee with all our powers of adoration.

CHRISTINA ROSSETTI,
1830-1894, British poet, lyricist

*J*ULY 25

JULY 26

*A*llow your dreams a place in your prayers and plans. God-given dreams can help you move into the future He is preparing for you.

BARBARA JOHNSON,
Contemporary, American writer, speaker

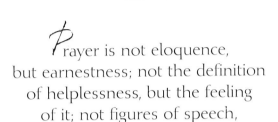

*P*rayer is not eloquence,
but earnestness; not the definition
of helplessness, but the feeling
of it; not figures of speech,
but earnestness of soul.

HANNAH MORE,
1745-1833, British writer, social reformer

*Don't be weary in prayer; keep at it; watch for
God's answers, and remember to be thankful
when they come.*

COLOSSIANS 4:2 TLB

JULY 27

July 28

From the world we see, hear, and touch, we behold inspired visions that reveal God's glory. In the sun's light, we catch warm rays of grace and glimpse His eternal design. In the birds' song, we hear His voice and it reawakens our need of Him. At the wind's touch, we feel His Spirit and sense our eternal existence.

WENDY MOORE,
1971- , American writer

Don't let controversy hurt your soul. Live near to God by prayer. Just fall down at His feet and open your very soul before Him, and throw yourself right into His arms.

CATHERINE BOOTH,
*1829-1890, British evangelist, first woman
Salvation Army general*

JULY 29

July 30

Just pray for a tough hide
and a tender heart.

RUTH BELL GRAHAM,
1920- , American writer, m. Billy Graham

$H$is tenderness in the springing grass,
His beauty in the flowers,
His living love in the sun above—
All here, and near, and ours.

CHARLOTTE PERKINS GILMAN,
1860-1935, American writer, social critic

JULY 31

August 1

*M*any persons have a wrong idea
of what constitutes real happiness.
It is not obtained through
self-gratification, but through
fidelity to a worthy purpose.

HELEN KELLER,
1919-1985, American writer, crusader for the handicapped

*To enjoy your work and to accept your lot
in life—that is indeed a gift from God.*

ECCLESIASTES 5:20 TLB

Life is not intended to be simply a round of work, no matter how interesting and important that work may be. A moment's pause to watch the glory of a sunrise or a sunset is soul satisfying, while a bird's song will set the steps to music all day long.

LAURA INGALLS WILDER,
1867-1957, American children's writer

August 2

AUGUST 3

People say, "What is the sense of our small effort?" They cannot see that we must lay one brick at a time, take one step at a time.

DOROTHY DAY,
1897-1980, American writer, social reformer

It's easy to be independent when you've got money. But to be independent when you haven't got a thing—that's the Lord's test.

MAHALIA JACKSON,
1911-1972, American gospel singer

AUGUST 4

AUGUST 5

Love is something like the clouds that were in the sky before the sun came out. You cannot touch the clouds, you know; but you feel the rain and know how glad the flowers and the thirsty earth are to have it after a hot day. You cannot touch love either; but you feel the sweetness that it pours into everything.

ANNIE SULLIVAN,
*1866-1936, American educator,
noted as Helen Keller's teacher*

*H*appiness comes of the capacity to feel deeply, to enjoy simply, to think freely, to risk life, to be needed.

STORM (MARGARET) JAMESON,
1891-1986, British writer

The Lord your God...will take great delight in you, he will quiet you with his love, he will rejoice over you with singing.

ZEPHANIAH 3:17 NIV

*A*UGUST 6

AUGUST 7

Choices can change our lives
profoundly. The choice to mend
a broken relationship, to say "yes"
to a difficult assignment, to lay aside
some important work to play
with a child, to visit some forgotten
person—these small choices may
affect many lives eternally.

GLORIA GAITHER,
Contemporary, American writer, singer/songwriter

$\mathcal{G}$od loves me as God loves all people, without qualification....
To be in the image of God means that all of us are made for the purpose of knowing and loving God and one another and of being loved in turn, not literally in the same way God knows and loves, but in a way appropriate to human beings.

ROBERTA BONDI,
Contemporary, American educator, writer

$\mathcal{A}$UGUST 8

AUGUST 9

We would have every arbitrary
barrier thrown down. We would
have every path laid open
to women as freely as to men.

MARGARET FULLER,
1810-1850, American writer

$\mathcal{A}$chievement is the knowledge
that you have studied and worked
hard and done the best that is in you.
Success is being praised by others,
and that's nice, too, but not as
important or satisfying. Always aim for
achievement and forget about success.

HELEN HAYES,
1900-1993, American actor

$\mathcal{A}$UGUST 10

AUGUST 11

*I*t is always possible to be thankful
for what is given rather than
to complain about what
is not given. One or the other
becomes a habit of life.

ELISABETH ELLIOT,
1926- , American writer,
m. martyred missionary Jim Elliot

In every thing give thanks.

1 THESSALONIANS 5:18 KJV

You must accept that you might fail; then, if you do your best and still don't win, at least you can be satisfied that you've tried. If you don't accept failure as a possibility, you don't set high goals, you don't branch out, you don't try—you don't take the risk.

ROSALYNN CARTER,
1927- , American First Lady

AUGUST 12

AUGUST 13

God...is greater than your problems. He can solve them all. Put your trust in Him and you will experience this.

BASILEA SCHLINK,
1904- , German nun, writer

*B*lessed are those who can
give without remembering
and take without forgetting.

ELIZABETH BIBESCO,
Contemporary, British writer, poet

*A*UGUST 14

$\mathcal{A}$UGUST 15

$\mathcal{I}$ would like to be known as a
person who is concerned about
freedom and equality and justice
and prosperity for all people.

ROSA PARKS,
1913- , American civil rights activist

Our Lord does not care so much for
the importance of our works as for
the love with which they are done.

TERESA OF AVILA,
1515-1582, Spanish Christian mystic, writer

*The ways of right-living people glow with
light; the longer they live, the brighter they
shine.... Keep vigilant watch over your heart;
that's where life starts.*

PROVERBS 4:18,23 THE MESSAGE

AUGUST 16

August 17

Money doesn't give you any
license to relax. It gives an
opportunity to use all your abilities,
free of financial worries, to go
forward, and to use your superior
advantages and talents to help others.

ROSE FITZGERALD KENNEDY,
1890-1995, mother of John F. Kennedy

*I*t is my calling to treat every human being with grace and dignity, to treat every person, whether encountered in a palace or a gas station, as a life made in the image of God.

SHEILA WALSH,
Contemporary, American singer, speaker

*A*UGUST 18

AUGUST 19

To follow without halt, one aim;
there is the secret of success. And
success? What is it? I do not find
it in the applause of the theater.
It lies rather in the satisfaction
of accomplishment.

ANNA PAVLOVA,
1881-1931, Russian ballerina

*F*ind the passion. It takes great
passion and great energy
to do anything creative. I would
go so far as to say you can't
do it without that passion.

AGNES DEMILLE,
1905- , American dancer, choreographer

*A*UGUST 20

*A*UGUST 21

*W*e never know how high we are
Till we are called to rise;
And then, if we are true to plan,
Our statures touch the skies.

EMILY DICKINSON,
1830-1886, American poet

*Finally...whatever is true, whatever
is honorable, whatever is right, whatever
is pure, whatever is lovely, whatever
is of good repute, if there is any excellence
and if anything worthy of praise,
let your mind dwell on these things.*

I long to put the experience of fifty years at once into your young lives, to give you at once the key to that treasure chamber every gem of which has cost me tears and struggles and prayers, but you must work for these inward treasures yourselves.

HARRIET BEECHER STOWE,
1811-1896, American writer

*A*UGUST 22

August 23

*E*xpressed affection is the best
of all methods to use when you
want to light a glow in someone's
heart and to feel it in your own.

RUTH STAFFORD PEALE,
1906- , American writer,
co-founder Foundation for Christian Living

All creatures have something visible and invisible. The visible is weak; the invisible is strong and alive. This [the invisible] seeks to get through to human understanding because human beings do not see it. And yet these invisible realities are forces in the workings of the Holy Spirit.

HILDEGARD OF BINGEN,
1098-1179, German nun, Christian mystic, poet

AUGUST 24

August 25

I share Einstein's affirmation that anyone who is not lost on the rapturous awe at the power and glory of the mind behind the universe "is as good as a burnt out candle."

MADELEINE L'ENGLE,
1918- , American writer

*T*he music soars within the little lark,
   And the lark soars.

ELIZABETH BARRETT BROWNING,
1806-1861, *British poet*

You have done so much for me, O Lord.
No wonder I am glad! I sing for joy.
O Lord, what miracles you do!
And how deep are your thoughts!

PSALM 92:4-5 TLB

*A*UGUST 26

AUGUST 27

The purpose of life, after all, is to live
it, to taste experience to the utmost,
to reach out eagerly without fear for
newer and richer experiences.

ELEANOR ROOSEVELT,
1884-1962, American First Lady, humanitarian

We don't need soft skies to make friendship a joy to us. What a heavenly thing it is; World without end, truly. I grow warm thinking of it, and should glow at the thought if all the glaciers of the Alps were heaped over me! Such friends God has given me in this little life of mine!

CELIA LAIGHTON THAXTER,
1835-1894, American poet

AUGUST 28

August 29

To be a joy-bearer and a joy-giver says everything, for in our life, if one is joyful, it means that one is faithfully living for God, and that nothing else counts; and if one gives joy to others one is doing God's work; with joy without and joy within, all is well....
I can conceive no higher way.

JANET ERSKINE STUART,
1857-1914, British member of Religious of the Sacred Heart

$\mathcal{G}$o outside, to the fields,
enjoy nature and the sunshine,
go out and try to recapture happiness
in yourself and in God. Think of all
the beauty that's still left in and
around you and be happy!

ANNE FRANK,
1929-1945, German Jewish diarist

$\mathcal{A}$UGUST 30

AUGUST 31

When we do what is right, we have contentment, peace, and happiness.

BEVERLY LAHAYE,
Contemporary, American writer

Knowing what is right is like a deep water in the heart; a wise person draws from the well within.

PROVERBS 20:5 THE MESSAGE

I never see what has been done;
I only see what remains to be done.

MARIE CURIE,
1867-1934, Polish-born French physicist

SEPTEMBER 1

SEPTEMBER 2

We are so preciously loved by God
that we cannot even comprehend it.
No created being can ever know
how much and how sweetly
and tenderly God loves them.

JULIAN OF NORWICH,
1342-1413, British Christian mystic

*f*aith and doubt both are needed—
not as antagonists, but working
side by side—to take
us around the unknown curve.

LILLIAN SMITH,
1897-1966, American educator, writer, social activist

SEPTEMBER 3

$\mathcal{S}$EPTEMBER 4

$\mathcal{F}$reedom is not the right
to do what we want but the power
to do what we ought.

CORRIE TEN BOOM,
1892-1983, Dutch evangelist, writer

*E*arth is crammed with heaven.

ELIZABETH BARRETT BROWNING,
1806-1861, British poet

*The Lord will guide you always; he will satisfy
your needs.... You will be like a well-watered
garden, like a spring whose waters never fail.*

ISAIAH 58:11 NIV

SEPTEMBER 5

SEPTEMBER 6

In all ranks of life the human heart yearns for the beautiful; and the beautiful things that God makes are His gift to all alike.

HARRIET BEECHER STOWE,
1811-1896, American writer

You pay God a compliment
by asking great things of Him.

TERESA OF AVILA,
1515-1582, Spanish Christian mystic, writer

SEPTEMBER 7

SEPTEMBER 8

My precious family and friends have taught me that joy and sorrow, storms and sunshine, tears and laughter are all part of living—and the sun does shine on the other side.

MARGARET JENSEN,
Contemporary, Canadian writer

*P*eople see God everyday,
they just don't recognize Him.

PEARL BAILEY,
1918-1990, American singer

SEPTEMBER 9

SEPTEMBER 10

The beauty of a woman is not
in a facial mole,
But true beauty in a woman
is reflected in her soul.
It is the caring that she lovingly gives,
the passion that she shows,
And the beauty of a woman with
passing years—only grows!

AUDREY HEPBURN,
1929-1993, Belgian actor

A kindhearted woman gains respect.

PROVERBS 11:16 NIV

$\mathcal{T}$he best reason to pray is that God is really there. In praying, our unbelief gradually starts to melt. God moves smack into the middle of even an ordinary day.... Prayer is a matter of keeping at it.... Thunderclaps and lightning flashes are very unlikely. It is well to start small and quietly.

EMILIE GRIFFIN,
Contemporary, American writer

$\mathcal{S}$EPTEMBER 11

SEPTEMBER 12

An effort made for
the happiness
of others lifts us
above ourselves.

LYDIA MARIE CHILD,
1802-1880, American abolitionist, writer

I like living. I have sometimes been wildly, despairingly, acutely miserable, racked with sorrow, but through it all I still know quite certainly that just to be alive is a grand thing.

AGATHA CHRISTIE,
1891-1975, British mystery writer, playwright

SEPTEMBER 13

SEPTEMBER 14

There can be no happiness
if the things we believe in are
different from the things we do.

FREYA MADELINE STARK,
1893-1993, British writer, traveler

Every one has a gift for
something, even if it is the
gift of being a good friend.

MARIAN ANDERSON,
1902-1993, *American singer*

*God has given each of you some special
abilities; be sure to use them
to help each other, passing on to others
God's many kinds of blessings.*

1 PETER 4:10 TLB

SEPTEMBER 15

SEPTEMBER 16

A soul cannot live without loving.
It must have something to love,
for it was created to love.

CATHERINE OF SIENA,
1347-1380, Italian Christian mystic

*T*he most important aspect is to be
yourself and have confidence in
yourself.... Triumph can't be had
without the struggle.

WILMA RUDOLPH,
1940-1994, American Olympic gold medalist

Our God gives you everything you need,
makes you everything you're to be.

2 THESSALONIANS 1:2 THE MESSAGE

*S*EPTEMBER 17

SEPTEMBER 18

*W*omen don't want a divided life....
They recognize that career
is not enough; they want to be
interconnected with people. They
want to keep growing throughout
their lives, adjusting as needed to
different circumstances. They want
to live a balanced life.

MARY ELLEN ASHCROFT,
1952- , American fiction writer

*G*od who is goodness and truth is also beauty. It is this innate human and divine longing, found in the company of goodness and truth, that is able to recognize and leap up at beauty and rejoice and know that all is beautiful, that there is not one speck of beauty under the sun that does not mirror back the beauty of God.

ROBERTA BONDI,
Contemporary, American educator, writer

SEPTEMBER 19

SEPTEMBER 20

There is no such thing as can't,
only won't. If you're qualified, all it
takes is a burning desire to
accomplish, to make a change. Go
forward, go backward. Whatever it
takes! But you can't blame other
people or society in general.
It all comes from your mind.
When we do the impossible we
realize we are special people.

JAN ASHFORD,
1932- , American businesswoman

*N*ot everyone possesses boundless energy or a conspicuous talent. We are not equally blessed with great intellect or physical beauty or emotional strength. But we have all been given the same ability to be faithful.

GIGI GRAHAM TCHIVIDJIAN,
1945- , American writer, speaker, d. Billy Graham

*S*EPTEMBER 21

SEPTEMBER 22

You don't just luck into things
as much as you'd like to think
you do. You build them
step by step, whether
it's friendships or opportunities.

BARBARA BUSH,
1925- , American First Lady

$\mathcal{W}$hat constitutes success? She has
achieved success who has lived well;
laughed often and loved much; who
has gained the respect of intelligent
people and the love of little children;
who has filled her niche and
accomplished her task; who has left
the world better than she found it;
who has always looked for the best in
others and given the best she had.

BESSIE ANDERSON STANLEY,
1904- , American writer

$\mathcal{S}$EPTEMBER 23

SEPTEMBER 24

When you are truly joined
in spirit, another woman's good
is your good too. You work for
the good of each other.

RUTH SENTER,
1944- , American writer

*I*ndividuals can change things....
If everyone will just do their little part,
then we can make a tremendous
difference in the lives of other people.

SARAH PURCELL,
1970- , American writer

*S*EPTEMBER 25

SEPTEMBER 26

One way or the other, God,
who thought up the family in the first
place, has the very best idea of how to
bring sense to the chaos of broken
relationships we see all around us.
I really believe that if I remain still
and listen a lot, He will share
some solutions with me so I can
share them with others.

JILL BRISCOE,
1935- , *American speaker, writer*

*H*ow we leave the world is more
important than how we enter it.

JANETTE OKE,
1935- , American writer

*May you be given more and more
of God's kindness, peace, and love.*

JUDE 1:2 TLB

*S*EPTEMBER 27

September 28

Gratitude unlocks the fullness of life. It turns what we have into enough, and more. It turns denial into acceptance, chaos to order, confusion to clarity. It can turn a meal into a feast, a house into a home, a stranger into a friend. Gratitude makes sense of our past, brings peace for today, and creates a vision for tomorrow.

Melody Beattie,
1948- , American writer, speaker

*G*od gave me my gifts.
I will do all I can
to show Him how
grateful I am to Him.

GRACE LIVINGSTON HILL,
1865-1947, American writer

SEPTEMBER 29

SEPTEMBER 30

*I*f I can think of myself as loved,
I can love and accept others.
If I see myself as forgiven, I can be
gracious toward others. If I see
myself as powerful, I can do what
I know is right. If I see myself as full,
I can give myself freely to others.

KATHY PEEL,
1951- , American writer

*I*t's simple things, like a glowing
sunset, the sound of a running stream
or the fresh smell in a meadow
that cause us to pause and marvel
at the wonder of life, to contemplate
its meaning and significance.
Who can hold an autumn leaf
in their hand, or sift the warm white
sand on the beach, and not wonder
at the Creator of it all?

WENDY MOORE,
1971- , American writer

*O*CTOBER 1

OCTOBER 2

Men judge us by the success
of our efforts. God looks
at the efforts themselves.

CHARLOTTE BRONTË,
1816-1855, British writer

Do you want to stand out? Then step down.
Be a servant. If you puff yourself up,
you'll get the wind knocked out of you.
But if you're content to simply be yourself,
your life will count for plenty.

MATTHEW 23:11-12 THE MESSAGE

$\mathcal{A}$s God's standard of everything is high, let us endeavor to live for Him with the highest intention in mind.

HANNAH MORE,
1745-1833, British writer, social reformer

$\mathcal{O}$CTOBER 3

OCTOBER 4

So often we think that to be encouragers we have to produce great words of wisdom when, in fact, a few simple syllables of sympathy and an arm around the shoulder can often provide much needed comfort.

FLORENCE LITTAUER,
1928- , American speaker, writer

It is not my business to think about myself. My business is to think about God. It is for God to think about me.

SIMONE WEIL,
1910-1943, French revolutionary, philosopher

OCTOBER 5

OCTOBER 6

When I look back at where
I've been, I see that what I am
becoming is a whole lot further
down the road from where I was.

GLORIA GAITHER,
Contemporary, American writer, singer/songwriter

*D*ear friends, I just dream
one day people all over the world
can live in real peace—no fighting,
and no hostility. We should work
together to build peace and happiness
for all people in all nations.

KIM PHUC,
1963- , Vietnam War survivor of Napalm bomb

Be of one mind, live in peace; and the
God of love and peace shall be with you.

2 CORINTHIANS 13:11 KJV

*O*CTOBER 7

OCTOBER 8

*I*f the world seems cold to you,
kindle fires to warm it.

LUCY LARCOM,
1824-1893, American editor, poet, mill worker

Often I have made a request
of God with earnest pleadings even
backed up with Scripture, only
to have Him say "No" because
He had something better in store.

RUTH BELL GRAHAM,
1920- , American writer, m. Billy Graham

OCTOBER 9

OCTOBER 10

*N*o one can make you feel inferior
without your consent.

ELEANOR ROOSEVELT,
1884-1962, American First Lady, humanitarian

$\mathcal{G}$od has put into each of our
lives a void that cannot be
filled by the world. We may leave
God or put Him on hold, but He
is always there, patiently waiting
for us...to turn back to Him.

EMILIE BARNES,
1938- , American speaker, writer

$\mathcal{O}$CTOBER 11

OCTOBER 12

Here's the test of the reality of your faith: on whom does your life depend?

ELISABETH ELLIOT,
1926- , American writer,
m. martyred missionary Jim Elliot

Steep yourself in God-reality, God-initiative, God-provisions. You'll find all your everyday human concerns will be met. Don't be afraid of missing out. You're my dearest friends! The Father wants to give you the very kingdom itself.

LUKE 12:28 THE MESSAGE

You're not obligated to win.
You're obligated to keep
trying to do the best
you can every day.

MARION WRIGHT EDELMAN,
1937- , *American attorney, civil rights activist*

OCTOBER 13

OCTOBER 14

It is not the still calm of life, or in the repose of a specific situation, that great characters are formed.

ABIGAIL ADAMS,
1744-1818, American First Lady

$\mathscr{A}$ woman is like a teabag;
you can't tell how strong she
is until you put her in hot water.

NANCY REAGAN,
1923- , American First Lady, actor

$\mathscr{O}$CTOBER 15

OCTOBER 16

People see God every day.
They just don't recognize Him.

PEARL BAILEY,
1918-1990, American singer

*T*he true way of softening one's troubles is to solace those of others.

MADAME DE MAINTENON,
1635-1719, French queen

Our hearts ache, but at the same time we have the joy of the Lord. We are poor, but we give rich spiritual gifts to others. We own nothing, and yet we enjoy everything.

2 CORINTHIANS 6:10 TLB

*O*CTOBER 17

OCTOBER 18

There is nothing so kingly as kindness,
And nothing so royal as truth.

ALICE CARY,
1820-1871, American poet

Life begets life. Energy creates
energy. It is by spending oneself
that one becomes rich.

SARAH BERNHARDT,
1844-1923, *French actor*

OCTOBER 19

OCTOBER 20

You have to look for the joy. Look for the light of God that is hitting your life, and you will find sparkles you didn't know were there.

BARBARA JOHNSON,
Contemporary, American writer, speaker

We have all known the long
loneliness and we have learned
that the only solution is love and that
love comes with community.

DOROTHY DAY,
1897-1980, American writer, social reformer

*O*CTOBER 21

OCTOBER 22

The well of Providence is deep.
It's the buckets we bring
to it that are small.

MARY WEBB,
1882-1927, Scottish religious leader, writer, poet

May your roots go down deep into the soil of
God's marvelous love; and may you be able to
feel and understand...how long, how wide,
how deep and how high His love really is.

EPHESIANS 3:17-18 TLB

*I*n order to realize the worth
of the anchor, we need
to feel the stress of the storm.

CORRIE TEN BOOM,
1892-1983, Dutch evangelist, writer

*O*CTOBER 23

OCTOBER 24

Real education should educate us out of self into something far finer—into a selflessness which links us with all humanity.

LADY NANCY ASTOR,
1879-1964, British, first woman Member of Parliament

$\mathcal{A}$s a mother, my job is to take
care of what is possible and trust
God with the impossible.

RUTH BELL GRAHAM,
1920- , American writer, m. Billy Graham

$\mathcal{O}$CTOBER 25

$\mathcal{O}$CTOBER 26

$\mathcal{S}$pread love everywhere you go:
first of all in your own home. Give
love to your children, to a wife or
husband, to a next-door neighbor.

MOTHER TERESA OF CALCUTTA,
1910-1997, Roman Catholic nun, Nobel Peace Prize winner

Some people regard discipline as a chore. For me, it is a kind of order that sets me free to fly.

JULIE ANDREWS,
1934- , British singer, actor

So, chosen by God for this new life of love, dress in the wardrobe God picked out for you: compassion, kindness, humility, quiet strength, discipline.

COLOSSIANS 3:12 THE MESSAGE

OCTOBER 27

$\mathcal{O}$CTOBER 28

$\mathcal{W}$hether we are poets or parents or teachers or artists or gardeners, we must start where we are and use what we have. In the process of creation and relationship, what seems mundane and trivial may show itself to be holy, precious, part of a pattern.

LUCI SHAW,
1928- , American writer

$\mathcal{H}$ow wonderful it is that nobody
need wait a single moment before
starting to improve the world.

ANNE FRANK,
1929-1945, German Jewish diarist

$\mathcal{O}$CTOBER 29

OCTOBER 30

It is an extraordinary and beautiful
thing that God, in creation...
works with the beauty of matter;
the reality of things; the discoveries
of the senses, all five of them;
so that we, in turn, may hear the grass
growing; see a face springing to life in
love and laughter.... The offerings of
creation...our glimpses of truth.

MADELEINE L'ENGLE,
1918- , American writer

We are each other's harvest; we are each other's business; we are each other's magnitude and bond.

GWENDOLYN BROOKS,
1917- , American poet, writer

OCTOBER 31

November 1

*F*aith has to be exercised in the midst
of ordinary, down-to-earth living.

ELISABETH ELLIOT,
1926- , American writer,
m. martyred missionary Jim Elliot

$\mathcal{G}$od is every moment totally aware
of each one of us. Totally aware in
intense concentration and love....
No one passes through any area
of life, happy or tragic, without the
attention of God with him.

EUGENIA PRICE,
1916-1996, American writer

$\mathcal{N}$OVEMBER 2

November 3

Let us love so well our work shall still be sweeter for our love, and still our love be sweeter for our work.

ELIZABETH BARRETT BROWNING,
1806-1861, *British poet*

*O*pinion is a flitting thing,
But Truth outlasts the Sun—
If then we cannot own them both—
Possess the oldest one.

EMILY DICKINSON,
1830-1886, American poet

I have chosen the way of truth;
I have set my heart on your laws....
I run in the path of your commands,
for you have set my heart free.

PSALM 119:30,32 NIV

*N*OVEMBER 4

November 5

*E*ncouragement is being a good listener, being positive, letting others know you accept them for who they are. It is offering hope, caring about the feelings of another, understanding.

Gigi Graham Tchividjian,
1945- , American writer, speaker, d. Billy Graham

*T*here is this important difference
between love and friendship:
while the former delights
in extremes and opposites,
the latter demands equalities.

MADAME DE MAINTENON,
1635-1719, French queen

*N*OVEMBER 6

November 7

If it is God who gives prayer,
then God often gives it in the form
of gratitude, and gratitude itself,
when it is received attentively in
prayer, is healing to the heart. Prayer
is such a mysterious business for
something so ordinary and everyday.

ROBERTA BONDI,
Contemporary, American educator, writer

*I*deal conversation must be an
exchange of thought, and not,
as many of those who worry most
about their shortcomings believe,
an eloquent exhibition of wit or oratory.

EMILY POST,
1873-1960, American writer, socialite

*N*OVEMBER 8

November 9

*Miracles are instantaneous,
they cannot be summoned,
but come of themselves, usually
at unlikely moments and
to those who least expect them.*

KATHERINE ANNE PORTER,
1890-1980, American writer

*He performs wonders that cannot be fathomed,
miracles that cannot be counted.*

JOB 5:9 NIV

A child her wayward pencil drew
On margins of her book;
Garlands of flower, dancing elves,
Bud, butterfly, and brook,
Lessons undone, and plum forgot,
Seeking with hand and heart
The teacher whom she learned to love
Before she knew t'was Art.

LOUISA MAY ALCOTT,
1832-1888, American writer

*N*OVEMBER 10

November 11

So wait before the Lord. Wait in the stillness. And in that stillness, assurance will come to you. You will know that you are heard; you will know that your Lord ponders the voice of your humble desires; you will hear quiet words spoken to you yourself, perhaps to your grateful surprise and refreshment.

AMY CARMICHAEL,
1867-1951, Irish missionary to India, poet

Life is either a daring adventure
or nothing at all. Security
is mostly a superstition.
It does not exist in nature.

HELEN KELLER,
1919-1985, American writer, crusader for the handicapped

NOVEMBER 12

November 13

What is success? I think
it is a mixture of having a flair
for the thing that you are doing;
knowing that it is not enough,
that you have got to have hard work
and a certain sense of purpose.

MARGARET THATCHER,
1925- , former Prime Minister of Great Britain

*W*e can do no great things, only
small things with great love.

MOTHER TERESA OF CALCUTTA,
1910-1997, Roman Catholic nun,
Nobel Peace Prize winner

So, chosen by God for this new life of love,
dress in the wardrobe God picked
out for you: compassion, kindness,
humility, quiet strength, discipline.

COLOSSIANS 3:12 THE MESSAGE

*N*OVEMBER 14

November 15

For women there are, undoubtedly,
  great difficulties in the path,
but so much the more to overcome.
  First, no woman should say,
"I am but a woman!" But a woman!
  What more can you ask to be?

MARIA MITCHELL,
1818-1889, American astronomer, educator

Oh, the comfort—the inexpressible comfort of feeling safe with a person—having neither to weigh thoughts nor measure words, but pouring them all right out, just as they are, chaff and grain together; certain that a faithful hand will take and sift them, keep what is worth keeping, and then with the breath of kindness blow the rest away.

DINAH MARIA MULOCK CRAIK, 1826-1887, *English writer*

NOVEMBER 16

NOVEMBER 17

I thank God that…[He] has raised up for Himself a people who are acting, in no small degree, up to the light which they have received.

CATHERINE BOOTH,
*1829-1890, British evangelist,
first woman Salvation Army general*

If you surrender completely
to the moments as they pass,
you live more richly those moments.

ANNE MORROW LINDBERGH,
1906-2001, American writer; m. Charles Lindbergh

*N*OVEMBER 18

November 19

For what I have received may the
Lord make me truly thankful.
And more truly for what
I have not received.

STORM (MARGARET) JAMESON,
1891-1986, British writer

*God can pour on the blessings
in astonishing ways so that you're ready
for anything and everything.*

2 CORINTHIANS 9:8 THE MESSAGE

*P*arents can only give good advice
or put them on the right paths,
but the final forming of a person's
character lies in their own hands.

ANNE FRANK,
1929-1945, German Jewish diarist

*N*OVEMBER 20

NOVEMBER 21

$\mathcal{G}$od's designs regarding you,
and His methods of bringing about
these designs, are infinitely wise.

MADAME JEANNE GUYON,
1648-1717, French Christian mystic

*I*t does not so much matter
what happens. It is what one does
when it happens that really counts.

LAURA INGALLS WILDER,
1867-1957, American children's writer

*N*OVEMBER 22

November 23

Taking joy in life is a woman's best cosmetic.

ROSALIND RUSSELL,
1911-1976, American actor

Instead of looking at the fashions, walk out into the fields and look at the wildflowers. They never primp or shop, but have you ever seen color and design quite like it?… If God gives such attention to the appearance of wild-flowers…don't you think he'll attend to you?

MATTHEW 6:28-30 THE MESSAGE

*P*lease know that I am aware
of the hazards. I want to do it because
I want to do it. Women must try
to do things as men have tried.
When they fail, their failure must
be a challenge to others.

AMELIA EARHART,
1897-1937, American aviator, writer

*N*OVEMBER 24

NOVEMBER 25

*F*aith is the first factor in a life devoted to service. Without faith, nothing is possible. With it, nothing is impossible.

MARY McLEOD BETHUNE,
1875-1955, American educator, writer

I learned three important things
in college—to use a library, to
memorize quickly and visually,
to drop asleep at any time given a
horizontal surface and fifteen
minutes. What I could not learn
was to think creatively on schedule.

AGNES DEMILLE,
1905- , American dancer, choreographer

*N*OVEMBER 26

NOVEMBER 27

*W*ere there no God we would be
in this glorious world with grateful
hearts and no one to thank.

CHRISTINA ROSSETTI,
1830-1894, British poet, lyricist

$\mathcal{G}$ratitude is the memory of the
heart; therefore forget not to say
often, I have all I ever enjoyed.

LYDIA MARIE CHILD,
1802-1880, American abolitionist, writer

Oh, give thanks to the Lord, for he is good;
His love and his kindness go on forever.

1 CHRONICLES 16:34 TLB

$\mathcal{N}$OVEMBER 28

NOVEMBER 29

I pray hard, work hard
and leave the rest to God.

FLORENCE GRIFFITH JOYNER,
1959- , American track athlete

*T*radition gives us a sense
of solidarity and roots,
a knowing there are some
things one can count on.

GLORIA GAITHER,
Contemporary, American writer, singer/songwriter

*N*OVEMBER 30

DECEMBER 1

*T*o be rooted is perhaps the most important and least recognized need of the human soul.

SIMONE WEIL,
1910-1943, French revolutionary, philosopher

*P*rayer is the deliberate
and persevering action of the soul.
It is true and enduring, and full of
grace. Prayer fastens the soul to God
and makes it one with God's will.

JULIAN OF NORWICH,
1342-1413, British Christian mystic

*D*ECEMBER 2

DECEMBER 3

For attractive lips,
Speak words of kindness.
For lovely eyes,
Seek out the good in people.
For a slim figure,
Share your food with the hungry.
For beautiful hair,
Let a child run his or her fingers
through it once a day.
For poise,
Walk with the knowledge
you'll never walk alone.

AUDREY HEPBURN,
1929-1993, Belgian actor

*T*ruth is always exciting. Speak it,
then. Life is dull without it.

PEARL S. BUCK,
1892-1973, American writer, Nobel Prize winner

*What you say goes, God, and stays,
as permanent as the heavens. Your truth
never goes out of fashion; it's up-to-date
as the earth when the sun comes up. Your
Word and truth are dependable as ever.*

PSALM 119:89-91 THE MESSAGE

*D*ECEMBER 4

 ECEMBER 5

*O*ne of the most wonderful things
about knowing God is that there's
always so much more to know,
so much more to discover. Just when
we least expect it, He intrudes
into our neat and tidy notions about
who He is and how He works.

JONI EARECKSON TADA
1950- , American writer, speaker

*T*uck [this] thought into your heart today. Treasure it. Your Father God cares about your daily everythings that concern you.

KAY ARTHUR,
1933- , American writer

*D*ECEMBER 6

DECEMBER 7

I see God as all-perfect, all-complete, all-powerful. God is love. I believe man is created in God's image. It makes a difference in a novel whether the writer believes we are created in God's image or whether we create God in our own.

FLANNERY O'CONNOR,
1925-1964, American writer

Genius is the gold in the mine;
talent is the miner that
works and brings it out.

LADY MARGUERITE BLESSINGTON,
1789-1849, British writer

DECEMBER 8

DECEMBER 9

*S*o where do you go when you
can't fix your life? The only place to go
is back to the One who made you.

SHEILA WALSH,
Contemporary, American singer, speaker

Pray to the Father. He loves to help.
You'll get his help, and won't be
condescended to when you ask for it.
Ask boldly, believing,
without a second thought.

JAMES 1:5-6 THE MESSAGE

Yes, I have doubted. I have wandered off the path. I have been lost. But I always returned. It is beyond the logic I seek. It is intuitive—an intrinsic, built-in sense of direction. I seem always to find my way home. My faith has wavered but has saved me.

HELEN HAYES,
1900-1993, American actor

DECEMBER 10

DECEMBER 11

Reach out and care for someone
who needs the touch of hospitality.
The time you spend caring
today will be a love gift that
will blossom into the fresh joy
of God's Spirit in the future.

EMILIE BARNES,
Contemporary, American writer

*I*f God sends us on stony paths,
He provides strong shoes.

CORRIE TEN BOOM,
1892-1983, Dutch evangelist, writer

*D*ECEMBER 12

DECEMBER 13

*C*herish your human
connections: your relationships
with friends and family.

BARBARA BUSH,
1925- , American First Lady

*I*f facts are the seeds that later
produce knowledge and wisdom,
then the emotions and the
impressions of the senses are
the fertile soil in which
the seeds must grow.

RACHEL CARSON,
1907-1964, American biologist, writer

*Listen…be wise, and keep your
heart on the right path.*

PROVERBS 23:19 NIV

*D*ECEMBER 14

DECEMBER 15

*C*haracter cannot be developed
in ease and quiet. Only through
experience of trial and suffering
can the soul be strengthened,
vision cleared, ambition inspired,
and success achieved.

HELEN KELLER,
1919-1985, American writer, crusader for the handicapped

*P*rayer is such an ordinary, everyday, mundane thing. Certainly, people who pray are no more saints than the rest of us. Rather, they are people who want to share a life with God, to love and be loved, to speak and to listen, to work and to be at rest in the presence of God.

ROBERTA BONDI,
Contemporary, American educator, writer

*D*ECEMBER 16

DECEMBER 17

*C*ertain springs are tapped
only when we are alone.... Women
need solitude in order to find again
the true essence of themselves;
that firm strand which will be the
indispensable center of a whole
web of human relationships.

ANNE MORROW LINDBERGH,
1906-2001, American writer; m. Charles Lindbergh

*T*he future belongs to those who
believe in the beauty of their dreams.

ELEANOR ROOSEVELT,
1884-1962, American First Lady, humanitarian

*No eye has seen, nor ear heard,
nor the human heart conceived, what God
has prepared for those who love him.*

1 CORINTHIANS 2:9 NRSV

*D*ECEMBER 18

DECEMBER 19

*T*his is the real gift: we have been
given the breath of life, designed with
a unique, one-of-a-kind soul that
exists forever—whether we live
it as burden or a joy or with
indifference doesn't change
the fact that we've been given
the gift of being now and forever.
Priceless in value, we are handcrafted
by God, who has a personal design
and plan for each one of us.

WENDY MOORE,
1971- , American writer

*C*hristmas, my child, is love in action.... When you love someone, you give to them, as God gives to us. The greatest gift He ever gave was the person of His Son, sent to us in human form so that we might know what God the Father is really like! Every time we love, every time we give, it's Christmas.

DALE EVANS ROGERS,
1912-2001, American actor, m. Roy Rogers

*D*ECEMBER 20

DECEMBER 21

We expect too much at Christmas.
It's got to be magical. It's got
to go right. Feasting. Fun.
The perfect present. All that
anticipation. Take it easy. Love's
the thing. The rest is tinsel.

PAM BROWN,
1948- , Australian writer

$\mathcal{G}$od grant you the light in
Christmas, which is faith;
the warmth of Christmas,
which is love…the all
of Christmas, which is Christ.

WILDA ENGLISH,
Writer

We all live off his generous bounty,
gift after gift after gift….
this exuberant giving and receiving,
This endless knowing and understanding—
all this came through Jesus, the Messiah.

JOHN 1:16-17 THE MESSAGE

$\mathcal{D}$ECEMBER 22

DECEMBER 23

*G*od must have said, "I know what I'll do, I'll send my LOVE right down there where they are. And I'll send it as a tiny baby, so they'll have to touch it, and they'll have to hold it close."

GLORIA GAITHER,
Contemporary, American writer, singer/songwriter

*A*ngels and archangels may have
gathered there,
Cherubim and seraphim
thronged the air;
But his mother only,
in her maiden bliss,
Worshipped the Beloved
with a kiss.

CHRISTINA ROSSETTI,
1830-1894, British poet, lyricist

*D*ECEMBER 24

DECEMBER 25

The coming of Jesus at Bethlehem brought joy to the world and to every human heart. May His coming this Christmas bring to each one of us that peace and joy that He desires to give.

MOTHER TERESA OF CALCUTTA,
*1910-1997, Roman Catholic nun,
Nobel Peace Prize winner*

*W*hen we put people before
possessions in our hearts,
we are sowing seeds
of enduring satisfaction.

BEVERLY LaHAYE,
Contemporary, American writer

DECEMBER 26

DECEMBER 27

*G*od's gifts put man's best
dreams to shame.

ELIZABETH BARRETT BROWNING,
1806-1861, British poet

*Let us not get tired of doing what
is right, for after a while we will
reap a harvest of blessing.*

GALATIANS 6:9 TLB

*W*holehearted, ready laughter heals, encourages, relaxes anyone within hearing distance. The laughter that springs from love makes wide the space around it—gives room for the loved one to enter in. Real laughter welcomes, and never shuts out.

EUGENIA PRICE,
1916-1996, American writer

*D*ECEMBER 28

ᗪECEMBER 29

If I can stop one heart from breaking,
I shall not live in vain:
If I can ease one life the aching,
Or cool one pain,
Or help one fainting robin
Unto his nest again,
I shall not live in vain.

EMILY DICKINSON,
1830-1886, American poet

Live for today but hold your hands open to tomorrow. Anticipate the future and its changes with joy. There is a seed of God's love in every event, every circumstance, every unpleasant situation in which you may find yourself.

BARBARA JOHNSON,
Contemporary , American writer, speaker

DECEMBER 30

December 31

I said to a man who stood at the gate of the year, "Give me a light that I may tread safely into the unknown." And he replied, "Go out into the darkness and put your hand in the hand of God. That shall be to you better than a light and safer than a known way."

M. Louise Haskins,
1875-1957, British writer, lecturer;
reply by King George VI